What Was
the Renaissance?

W0081793

by Roberta Edwards

illustrated by Gregory Copeland

Penguin Workshop

To Jill Abramson, a Renaissance Woman—RE

For Megan and Ryan—GC

PENGUIN WORKSHOP
An imprint of Penguin Random House LLC
1745 Broadway, New York, New York 10019

First published in the United States of America by Penguin Workshop,
an imprint of Penguin Random House LLC, 2025

Copyright © 2025 by Penguin Random House LLC

Penguin Random House values and supports copyright. Copyright fuels creativity,
encourages diverse voices, promotes free speech, and creates a vibrant culture. Thank you
for buying an authorized edition of this book and for complying with copyright laws by
not reproducing, scanning, or distributing any part of it in any form without permission.
You are supporting writers and allowing Penguin Random House to continue to publish
books for every reader. Please note that no part of this book may be used or reproduced in
any manner for the purpose of training artificial intelligence technologies or systems.

PENGUIN is a registered trademark and PENGUIN WORKSHOP is a trademark
of Penguin Books Ltd. WHO HQ & Design is a registered trademark
of Penguin Random House LLC.

Visit us online at penguinrandomhouse.com.

Library of Congress Cataloging-in-Publication Data is available.

Printed in the United States of America

ISBN 9780593751831 (paperback)   10 9 8 7 6 5 4 3 2 1 CJKW
ISBN 9780593751848 (library binding)   10 9 8 7 6 5 4 3 2 1 CJKW

Contents

What Was the Renaissance? 1

A New Way of Thinking 6

The Miracle of Printing 17

A New Way of Painting 22

Leonardo da Vinci, All-Around Genius . . . 30

Michelangelo, All-Around Genius 45

A New Way of Building 63

A Renaissance in the North 76

The Heavens Above 86

The World Grows Larger 94

A Giant Leap Forward 103

Timelines 106

Bibliography 108

What Was the Renaissance?

In early January 1506, a farmer was working in his vineyard on a hillside near the city of Rome. (A vineyard is an area of land where grapes for winemaking are grown.) Suddenly, he felt something hard in the ground. It wasn't a rock or a boulder but something much, much bigger.

He dug deeper and deeper. What was there? A marble statue that was more than eight feet tall.

The farmer did not know it, but the statue had been made about fifteen hundred years earlier during the period in history known as classical antiquity.

The statue was of a bearded man and his two sons struggling against giant sea serpents. Their faces showed terror, agony, desperation.

Laocoön and His Sons

Their bodies twisted and turned attempting to get free. Everything looked real. It was possible to imagine actual muscles and bones underneath the marble skin.

A famous sculptor heard about the farmer's discovery and went to see it. His name was Michelangelo. He wanted his own statues to look as lifelike as the one found at the vineyard. So did many other artists at the time.

In fact, all over Europe, there was renewed interest in ancient European cultures. It brought forth an explosion of creativity and new ideas—not only in art but in science, math, astronomy, and architecture. This period lasted from about 1400 to 1600. It became known as the Renaissance. In French that means "rebirth."

Yet the Renaissance didn't start in France. It started in Italy. The farmer's accidental discovery of an eight-foot-tall sculpture helps explain the reason why.

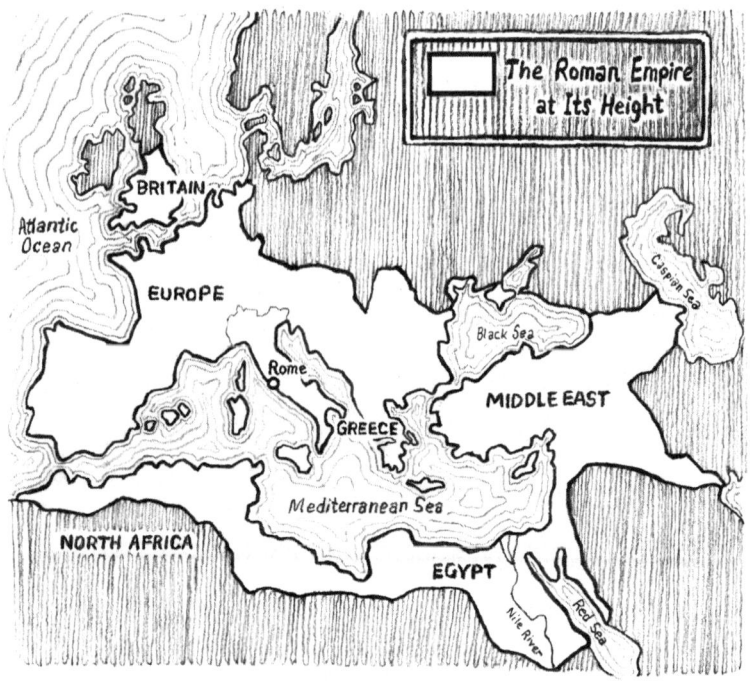

In ancient times, Rome was the center of a vast empire that for a time included Greece, the Middle East, northern Africa, and parts of Europe.

Even after the fall of the Roman Empire in 476 CE, reminders of its greatness were everywhere in the city of Rome. Sometimes they were still in plain sight, like the giant arena known as the

Colosseum, and the Pantheon, a temple to the Roman gods. Sometimes they lay buried right under people's feet. This is why a farmer working on his land as he did every day could stumble upon something extraordinary.

CHAPTER 1
A New Way of Thinking

During the Renaissance, there arose a new way to look at life and its meaning. It was called humanism. Its followers believed that people were basically good and could do great things.

Followers of humanism got many of their ideas from studying the written works of ancient Greek philosophers. (A philosopher is someone who seeks wisdom and the meaning of life.) The philosophers from the classical past, ancient Greece and Rome from about 800 BCE to 400 CE, believed people should strive to live a happy life and that they could judge for themselves what was right and wrong.

Until the dawn of the Renaissance around 1400, works by these philosophers had largely been forgotten. No one was reading them anymore. Still, scholars knew of their existence and so they began searching for them. Sometimes they found copies on the dusty shelves of old libraries. Sometimes travelers brought back copies from Constantinople. (Constantinople was the name for the city now known as Istanbul in Turkey.) It had remained a center of learning throughout the Middle Ages.

Art Before the Renaissance

The Middle Ages was a period that lasted from about 400 to 1400. During that time, the Catholic Church held tremendous power over almost everyone living in Western Europe. Paintings were meant to send a religious message. Seeing the figure of Jesus on the cross, for example, reminded Christians of their faith.

The names of artists from the Middle Ages are rarely known to us. They didn't sign their work because they weren't considered important enough to do so. They were merely craftsmen.

But during the Renaissance, artists were appreciated for their creativity. Some, like Leonardo da Vinci and Michelangelo, were recognized as geniuses.

The Crucifixion, c. 1330–1335

Who were some of the most famous Greek philosophers?

One was Socrates (c. 469–399 BCE). He lived in Athens, the capital of ancient Greece. He could usually be found in the marketplace, talking to people. He didn't give lectures. He liked to ask questions that made people think

Socrates

about truth, bravery, and justice. Socrates never wrote down anything. What is known about him comes from others. In 399 BCE, Socrates was sentenced to death for challenging beliefs about the Roman gods. Surrounded by friends, he was forced to drink a cup of poison called hemlock.

Plato (c. 427–347 BCE) was one of Socrates's

students. Plato started a school that met outdoors in Athens. He had many ideas about what made good government. His most famous work, *Republic*, is still taught in college classes today.

Plato

Aristotle (384–322 BCE) was a student of Plato's. He wrote that happiness was the meaning

Aristotle

and purpose of life. He thought that doing good deeds made people happy. He is known as the first scientist. The son of a doctor, Aristotle was very interested in anatomy (studying the human body).

As for the humanists, Francesco Petrarca (1304–1374) was the first. In English he is  called Petrarch. He was born in Arezzo, Italy, and encouraged scholars to read the works of ancient Greek philosophers. His father was a lawyer and wanted Petrarch to become one, too. Instead, he wrote poetry. Petrarch looked for and found many classical works, including volumes of letters written by a Roman philosopher named Cicero. Petrarch was such an admirer of Cicero's that he wrote letters to him as if they were friends. (By then, Cicero had been dead for way more than a thousand years.)

Francesco Petrarca

Leon Battista Alberti (1404–1472) was another humanist from northern Italy. He became famous as an author, artist, and architect. (He also liked inventing secret codes!) Alberti wanted the designs of new buildings to have columns, arches, and domes so they'd resemble ones from antiquity. His ideas influenced many of the artists and architects of the Renaissance.

The humanist Thomas More (1478–1535) was from London, England. He wrote a famous novel called *Utopia* about an imaginary island. No one there owned private property; all the food was shared. According to More, Utopia was the ideal place to live. In fact, today, the word *utopia* means "an earthly paradise."

Thomas More

For a time, Thomas More was the most important and valued adviser to King Henry VIII.

More also remained a faithful Catholic throughout his life. This eventually caused a terrible rift between himself and the king. Henry had decided that England would break away from the Catholic Church. Why? The pope (the head of the Church) would not allow the king to get a divorce.

So Henry started his own church—the Church of England—with himself as head of it. Thomas More, however, would not go along with the king. For angering the king, he paid a heavy price. The king had Thomas More beheaded in 1535.

From its beginnings in Italy, humanism spread quickly across Western Europe. Why did the movement catch on so rapidly? It was because of one invention: the printing press.

CHAPTER 2
The Miracle of Printing

It's hard to exaggerate the importance of the invention of the printing press. Beginning in the Renaissance, information could reach masses of people quickly. Like the internet in the late twentieth century, the printing press was a total game changer.

In the Middle Ages, there hadn't been many books. Every single one had to be copied out by hand. Word for word, sentence by sentence, page by page. Most books were about religion. It might take as long as a year for a scribe (the person doing the writing) to copy the entire Bible.

Because of how few books there were, they were very expensive. Only the rich and powerful could afford to own them. A king or emperor might pay to have a book made to order. It would usually include a calendar of the months and prayers for different times of the day. The buyer would also say how many illustrations there had

to be and whether they'd be in black and white or in color, which was much more expensive. Called illuminated manuscripts, these books are among the most treasured artworks from the Middle Ages.

Not much is known about the man who, around 1440, developed a machine for printing books. His name was Johannes Gutenberg and he lived in Mainz, Germany. He was a craftsman who made beautiful objects—goblets, candlesticks, and plates—from gold.

Why did Gutenberg want to make a printing press? Did he love to read? Did he want to own books himself? Did he see a chance to earn a lot of money?

No one knows.

Gutenberg was not the first to develop a way to print books. However, his machine was a big improvement over anything that had come before.

Johannes Gutenberg and his printing press

Gutenberg's new printing press made use of  what's called movable type— tiny blocks of metal, each with a raised letter on top. The blocks could be arranged in any way and used over and over again.

Words were made by putting the letter blocks in the proper order. A whole page of type would be fitted into a frame, laid on a platen (a flat piece of wood), and inked all over. Then a piece of paper was placed on the inked surface and another platen pressed down on it. The result was a single printed page.

Soon Gutenberg's press was producing three hundred pages a day. He printed so many copies of the Bible that it no longer cost all that much to buy one. Today, fewer than forty printed editions of the original Gutenberg Bibles still exist. Each is worth millions of dollars.

An original Gutenberg Bible

Just fifty years after the invention of the printing press, there were twenty million books in Europe! There were printing presses in all the big cities. Bookstores too. The availability of inexpensive books meant that many more people learned to read and hear about new ideas, including those of the Renaissance.

CHAPTER 3
A New Way of Painting

When people today hear the word *Renaissance*, it is unlikely that they first think of humanism or the printing press. What most often comes to mind are paintings, especially masterpieces by such artists as Leonardo da Vinci and Michelangelo.

There was a new style of art developing during the Renaissance. Painters began to depict realistic people in natural surroundings. That had not been true of paintings in the Middle Ages, when most art had been made for churches and castles. (The Middle Ages lasted from about 400 to 1400.) Medieval paintings depicted important events from the Bible. The faces of the figures have little expression. Bodies appear flat and seem to float in space. Buildings are so spindly, it looks like a light breeze would knock them over. That's because medieval artists were not trying to represent the real world.

A painting from the Middle Ages

The new style of painting started in the city-state of Florence, today part of Italy. (A city-state governs itself and is not part of any country.) It didn't happen overnight. It had been developing since the end of the thirteenth century.

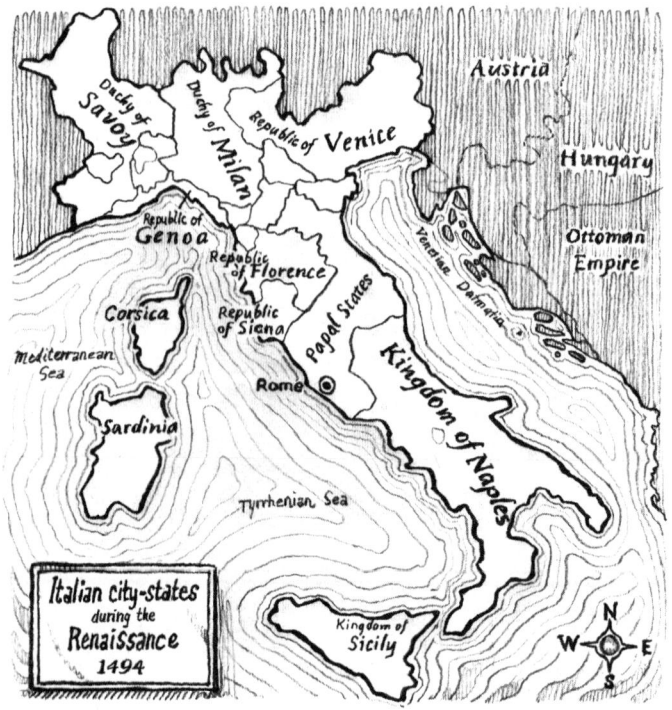

Italian city-states during the Renaissance 1494

Why Florence?

Florence was a forward-looking city, the birthplace of humanism, a center for new ideas. Florence was also a rich city. Wealthy merchant families were eager to spend money—often a lot of it!—on artwork. Owning paintings by the outstanding painters of the day showed off their own good taste.

Masaccio was a very gifted young painter in Florence. (In Italian, his name means Big Tom.) He worked in the 1420s, during what is called the Early Renaissance. Masaccio became famous for painting a series of large frescoes on the walls of a church in Florence. A fresco is a painting done directly on the wet plaster of a ceiling or a wall.

Masaccio (center) self-portrait, 1420

In one scene, an official of the Roman Empire (shown from the back) demands that Jesus pay taxes before entering the temple. Jesus is in the center, surrounded by his twelve followers.

Masaccio wanted the scene to be dramatic and imitate real life. He painted Jesus's followers with different expressions and gestures. They look extremely realistic, like flesh-and-blood people. As with all paintings, this was created on a flat two-dimensional surface. In this case, a wall.

Yet Masaccio used new techniques to achieve the illusion of depth—to make viewers think that what they were looking at was taking place in an actual three-dimensional space.

The techniques were based on principles of math and geometry first known in ancient Greece. Everything happening in the foreground (close to the viewer) needs to be shown much bigger than what's taking place farther back. This is exactly how our eyes see things. Painting objects in correct size to each other is called using proportion.

Detail of a fresco
by Masaccio

Another way Masaccio tried to create the illusion of real space was by adding shadows, showing natural sources of light, and using foreshortening—depicting only part of an object, the part a viewer sees from a certain angle. Think of a person pointing their finger right in front of you. You don't see their whole hand.

Mapping out the scene with angled lines meeting at a "vanishing point" meant Masaccio would paint everything in the correct perspective.

Masaccio's perspective

Think of train tracks. The sides always remain parallel—at an equal distance from each other. But for a picture of train tracks to look correct, the lines on both sides need to keep slanting inward, little by little, until they seem to meet in the far distance on the horizon.

Tragically, Masaccio had a very short career. He died when he was only twenty-seven. Had he lived longer, imagine what masterpieces he might have produced. He might have become as famous as Leonardo da Vinci and Michelangelo.

CHAPTER 4
Leonardo da Vinci, All-Around Genius

The term "Renaissance man" describes someone who is good at many different things. They have a variety of talents and a wide range of interests. The term perfectly describes Leonardo da Vinci.

As a child, he was curious about everything he

saw—a flowering plant, an insect, a pool of water. He hoped to one day write an encyclopedia of the entire world. Like many of his plans, however, it remained just an idea. Leonardo ranks among the most extraordinary artists who ever lived. Yet over a fifty-year-long career, he left only ten finished paintings. It seems he couldn't keep his mind on any one thing for long. He'd get distracted or bored or discouraged.

Born in 1452, Leonardo came from Vinci, a hilltop town outside Florence. He was handsome, funny, and a good athlete. Even when he was a young boy, his skill at drawing was remarkable. But he was a poor student; learning to read was difficult for him.

His father wasn't sure Leonardo would ever amount to much. However, he did notice Leonardo's artistic talent, and he began thinking that perhaps his son could become a painter. That was a respectable career. When Leonardo was twelve, his father arranged for him to become an apprentice to a famous artist in Florence. The artist's name was Verrocchio.

Leonardo would now live with him.

At this time, only boys could be apprentices. Their training took years. They started out by running errands and doing simple jobs in the workshop. They mixed paints and made paintbrushes. At the same time, they learned the basic skills of drawing and painting.

Sometimes after many years, an apprentice was allowed to complete a small part of a painting. In *The Baptism of Christ* by Verrocchio, Leonardo painted a dazzlingly beautiful little angel. It made the other figures look wooden and lifeless.

The Baptism of Christ by Verrocchio

One story says that after seeing Leonardo's little angel, Verrocchio realized his young apprentice was a far better artist than he was. He never picked up a paintbrush again.

After spending thirteen years in Verrocchio's workshop, Leonardo was ready to work on his own. He was given many commissions (contracts for jobs). But he angered clients by not finishing the work. When he did, it took him much too long.

Throughout his life, Leonardo was unreliable.

And his eagerness to experiment with new art techniques sometimes ended in disaster.

For the wall of a dining room, Leonardo created a dramatic fresco called *The Last Supper*. In this scene, Jesus sits at a long table surrounded by all twelve of his followers. He already knows that one of them is going to betray him.

Leonardo had never made a fresco before. A fresco painter works on only one small area of wet plaster at a time. Plaster dries fast so the painting needs to be done quickly. Mistakes can't be corrected. Leonardo liked to paint slowly and carefully. He liked being able to make changes. So he invented a new kind of paint with oil and egg in it. This allowed him to work at his own pace.

When completed, Leonardo's fresco was a marvel. People from all over the region came to see it. And it remains a highly visited site today.

There was a problem, however. A big problem. Leonardo's new paint didn't stick properly to the wall. After only twenty years, it started flaking off. Over the centuries, there have been many attempts to restore the fresco. Yet *The Last Supper* remains no more than a shadow of its original self.

Another project also ended unhappily. The duke of Milan, an important man in a powerful city-state north of Florence, hired Leonardo to make a gigantic bronze statue of a horse. The biggest one ever.

Leonardo was very excited. He completed a full-size, twenty-four-foot-tall model in clay. The bronze was ready for casting the actual statue. Then France went to war against Milan. The bronze was melted down for bullets and when French archers entered the city, they used Leonardo's clay horse for target practice. It was shot to bits!

Still, it wouldn't matter if Leonardo had left nothing to the world besides the Mona Lisa. Many people believe the portrait is of Lisa del Giocondo, the wife of a Florentine merchant.

Leonardo employed everything he knew about painting to bring Mona Lisa to life. Proportion, perspective, shading. He also invented a new trick. By blurring the lines between hills in the distance, they seem to slowly fade from view.

Leonardo loved the painting so much that he refused to sell it. For thirty years, he kept making little changes to it. The *Mona Lisa* was with him when he died in 1519, while staying in France as the guest of the French king. (That explains why the painting is still in France.)

What gave Leonardo the most pleasure was keeping illustrated notebooks of all his thoughts and ideas. For instance, he drew plans for inventions that only came into existence many hundreds of years later—flying machines, war tanks, a bicycle, a parachute, robots. Every little doodle—even of something as ordinary as a screw—is a delicate work of art.

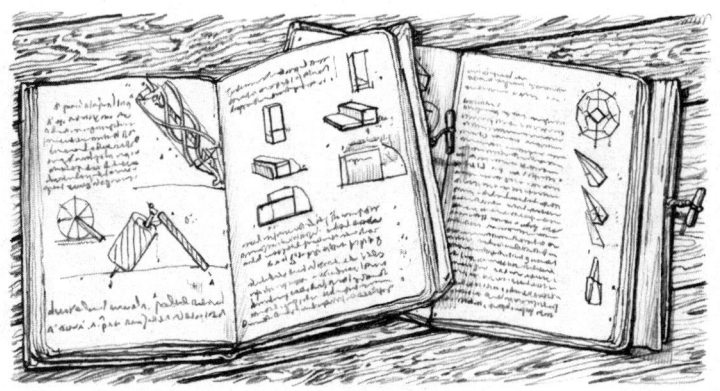

The Real Mona Lisa?

Many people believe the woman who sat for the most famous painting in the world is Lisa Gherardini (1479–1542). Lisa was born in Florence. She married Francesco del Giocondo in 1495, and

the couple had five children together.

Her portrait, the *Mona Lisa*, is one of the most valuable paintings in the world. It is on display in the Louvre Museum in Paris, where it was hung in 1804. The painting is visited by nearly ten million people each year!

Leonardo was especially curious about the human body and how it worked. The only way to examine them was to dissect (cut into) bodies of the dead. Although it was illegal, Leonardo paid grave robbers for bodies. By studying the muscles, bones, and organs, Leonardo came to know far more about anatomy than most doctors at the time. Using mathematical principles, Leonardo worked out the ideal proportions of a human body. He believed the height of a man should be the same as the width of both arms outstretched. Around 1490, Leonardo made a very famous drawing showing this.

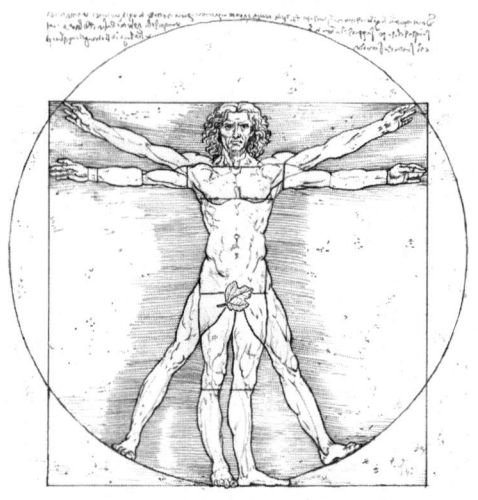

Mirror Writing

Leonardo da Vinci wrote backward, from right to left, in his notebooks. If a mirror is held up to the words, it is easy to read them. Did he use mirror writing to keep his ideas a secret? Maybe.

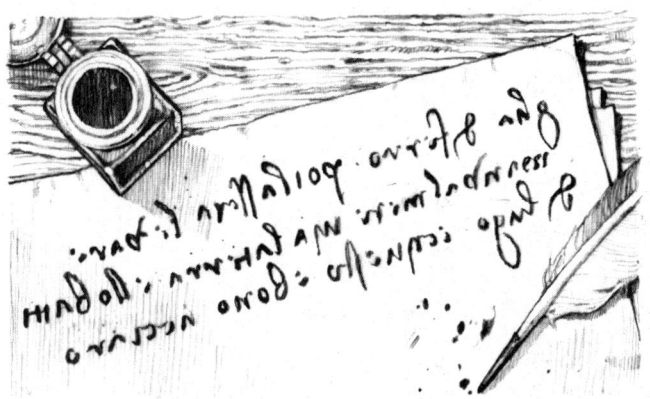

Leonardo da Vinci's backward handwriting

But maybe not. He was left-handed, so by writing this way, he avoided smearing the ink.

Unfortunately, after his death, pages from Leonardo's notebooks were torn out and sold individually. About seven thousand pages are accounted for. But perhaps as many as seven thousand more have vanished. In 1994, Bill Gates, the founder of Microsoft, bought a collection of thirty-six pages. He paid almost thirty-one million dollars for them!

VCG Wilson/Fine Art/Corbis Historical/Getty Images

Middle panel of the *Annunciation Triptych* by the workshop of
Robert Campin, 1427–1432

Electa/Mondadori Portfolio/Hulton Fine Art Collection/Getty Images

Adoration of the Mystic Lamb, a center panel of the Ghent Altarpiece, by Jan van Eyck and Hubert van Eyck, completed in 1432

Angelo Hornak/Corbis Historical/Getty Images

The Pazzi Chapel designed by Filippo Brunelleschi, 1420s–1430s

Dome ceiling of Florence Cathedral, completed in 1436

Julian Elliott Photography/Stone/Getty Images

DEA/G. DAGLI ORTI/De Agostini Editorial/Getty Images

Obsequies of St. Fina by Ghirlandaio, c. 1475

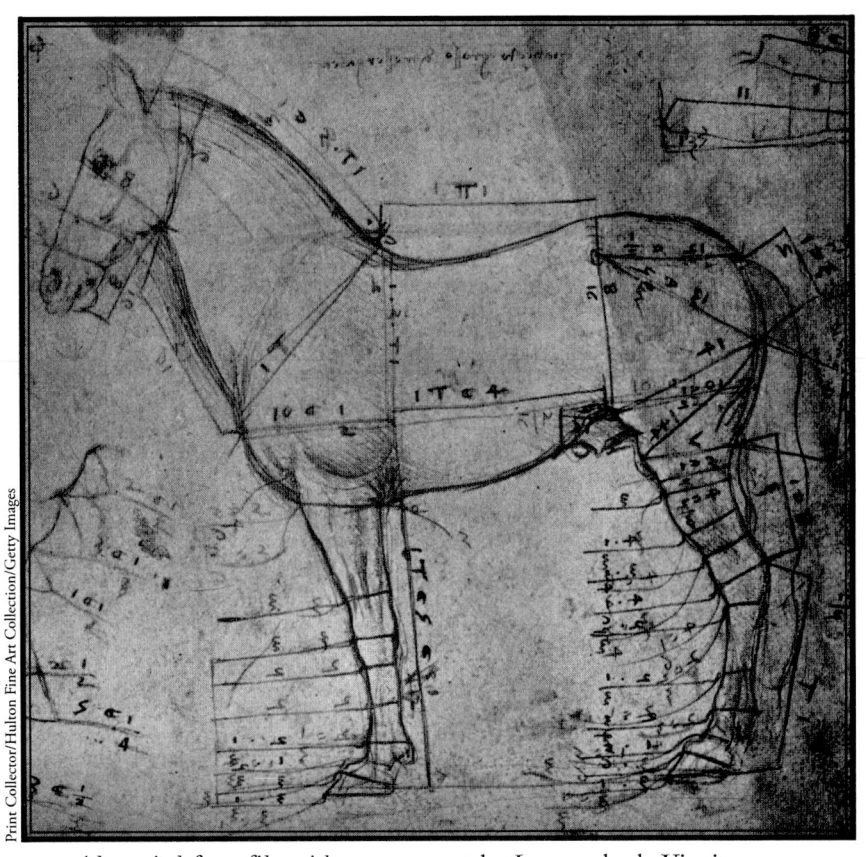

Print Collector/Hulton Fine Art Collection/Getty Images

A horse in left profile, with measurements by Leonardo da Vinci, c. 1490

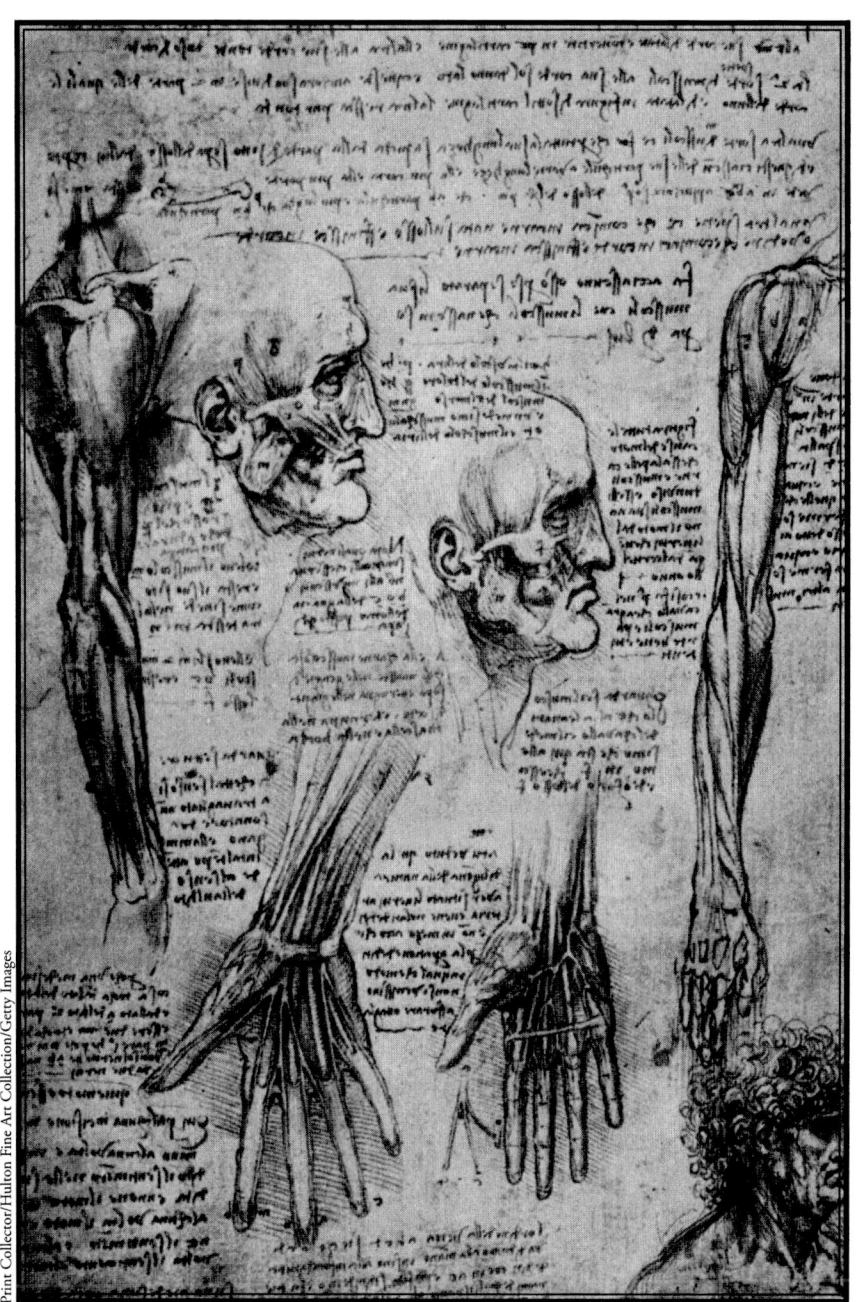

*Studies of the muscles of the face and arm, and the nerves and veins
of the hand* by Leonardo da Vinci, 1510–1511

Print Collector/Hulton Fine Art Collection/Getty Images

Laszlo Szirtesi/Getty Images News/Getty Images

Pietà by Michelangelo, 1499

Lucas Schifres/Getty Images News

The Deposition by Michelangelo, 1547–1555

Bettmann/Getty Images

Creation of the Sun, Moon, and Plants, part of the frescoes on the
Sistine Chapel ceiling, by Michelangelo, 1508–1512

Ashmolean Museum/Heritage Images/Hulton Fine Art Collection/Getty Images

Head of Bearded Man Shouting by Michelangelo, c. 1515

coverdale84/E+/Getty Images

Moses by Michelangelo, 1513–1515

ZU_09/DigitalVision Vectors/Getty Images

Printing press, 1520

Interior of the dome of St. Peter's Basilica,
designed by Michelangelo, mid-1550s

Pascal Deloche/Stone/Getty Images

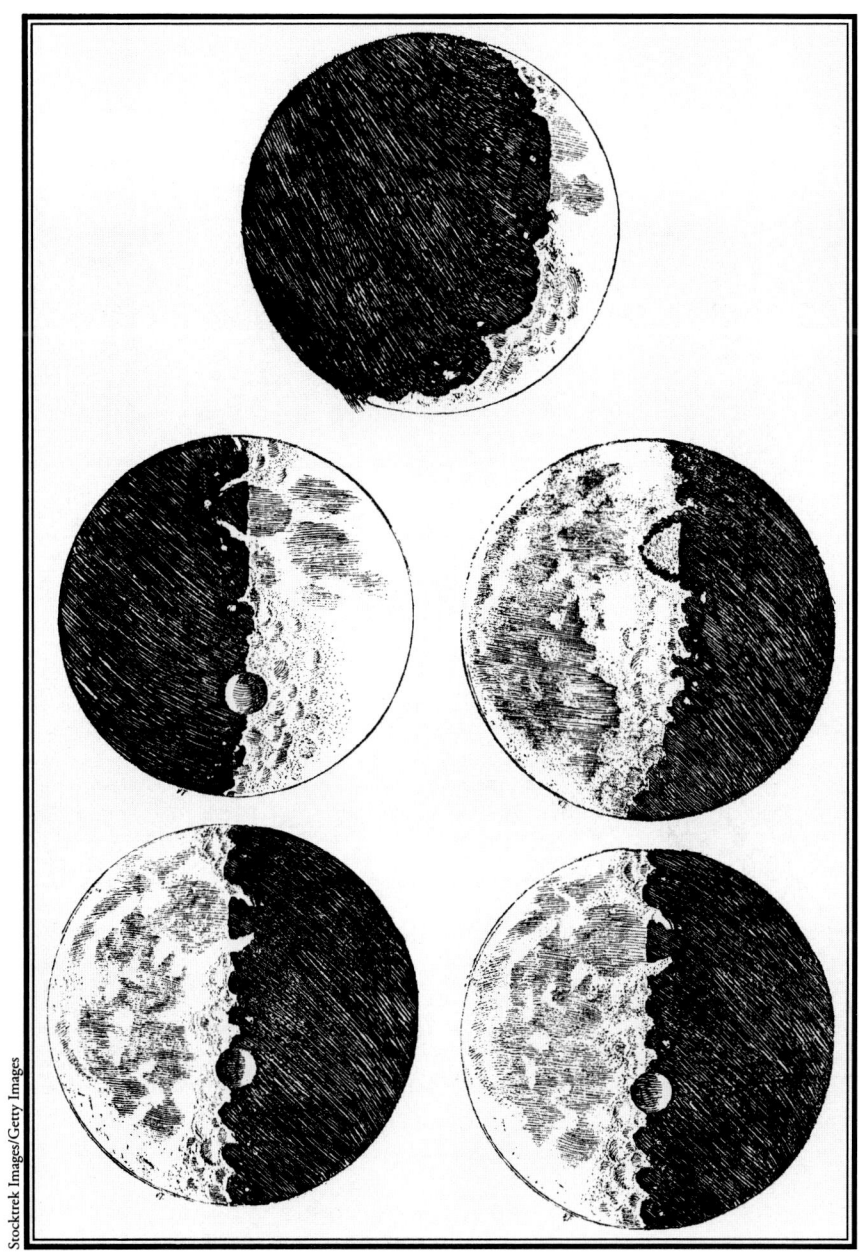

Illustrations of the phases of the moon by Galileo, 1609

Stocktrek Images/Getty Images

Vittoriano Rastelli/Corbis Historical/Getty Images

The Last Supper by Leonardo da Vinci,
1495–1498, being restored in 1986

CHAPTER 5
Michelangelo, All-Around Genius

Leonardo was one of the first celebrity artists, famous during his own lifetime.

Michelangelo was another. No last name is necessary to describe either of them.

These two giants of what is called the High Renaissance—the

Leonardo da Vinci

years from about 1490 to 1530—were nothing alike.

Leonardo was charming and well dressed and enjoyed the pleasures of life, such as music and parties and fine food. He was kindhearted, too. At the marketplace, he'd buy little birds in cages, then immediately set them free.

Michelangelo was known for wearing dirty clothes and rarely bathing. Once, after making a nasty remark to another man, Michelangelo got punched in the face! He ended up with a badly broken nose that you can see in portraits of the great artist. Whereas Leonardo was a dreamer, Michelangelo was a doer.

Michelangelo

He had almost superhuman drive. He'd become so obsessed with whatever he was working on that he'd forget to eat or sleep.

Not only were Leonardo and Michelangelo professional rivals, neither could stand the other.

Although he created world-famous frescoes in Rome, Michelangelo never thought of himself as a painter. (Leonardo didn't think he was a very good one. He said the oversize muscles on Michelangelo's people looked like big "bags of walnuts.")

First and foremost, Michelangelo considered himself a sculptor. He thought that was a far more noble and more difficult profession than being a painter. He would stare for hours at a block of stone until finally he saw the way to release "the soul" buried inside.

Michelangelo (1475–1564) could have led a comfortable life. He was from a well-off Florentine family, the Buonarrotis. Not long after he was born, his mother became sick. So he was sent to live with a nurse and her husband in a nearby village. The husband was a stonemason. He cut blocks of marble from the quarries nearby, which would be carved into statues. Young

Michelangelo was fascinated watching this work. It made him want to become a sculptor, someone using a hammer and chisels.

At age ten, he went back to Florence to live with his family. Like Leonardo, Michelangelo became an apprentice in the workshop of a famous artist. His name was Ghirlandaio.

Ghirlandaio was impressed with Michelangelo's talent right away. He sent him to the palace of the

Medicis, the richest and most powerful family in Florence at the time.

The Medici palace

In the courtyard of the Medici palace, the teenage boy carved copies of statues that had been created in ancient Greece. Lorenzo de' Medici, the head of the family, was impressed, too. Here before him was a born sculptor! He let Michelangelo spend three years living and working at the palace. Lorenzo treated him like a son.

In 1501, when he was only twenty-six, Michelangelo began work on what is one of the best-known statues in the world. It is of David, the biblical hero who killed a giant named Goliath.

The block of marble that Michelangelo used had been cut years before. However, two other sculptors had already refused to work with it. Michelangelo understood why. The piece of stone was an odd shape and size, too tall and too narrow. To Michelangelo this presented an interesting challenge.

The huge block had remained unused in a workshop for twenty years until Michelangelo decided to work with it.

According to the Bible story, a young shepherd named David managed to kill a giant with a single rock flung from his slingshot. Michelangelo had been to Rome and seen statues of Greek gods from ancient times. That's what he wanted his David to look like. Only much, much bigger. And so he created a statue that was seventeen feet tall, almost three times the height of an average person.

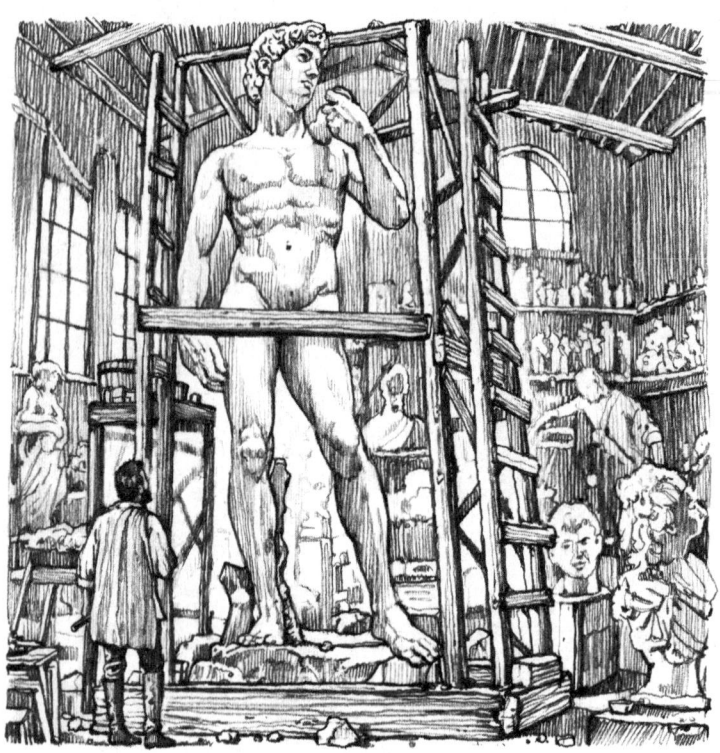

Michelangelo carved David in the nude—without any clothes on. The statue was free-standing, meaning a viewer could walk all the way around it. This required much greater skill than carving only the front of a statue that would be partly attached to a wall.

A Different David

Around 1435, a Florentine sculptor named Donatello (1386–1466) made the first nude, free-standing statue since ancient times.

Donatello's David, created nearly seventy years before Michelangelo's, was much smaller (only five feet, five inches) and made of bronze.

Donatello portrayed David as a younger teenager in a flowered helmet—not nearly as powerful looking as Michelangelo's hero.

Ordinarily statues of David showed him after his victory. Michelangelo, however, chose to

depict the moment before David delivers the fatal blow. The slingshot is still over his shoulder. The rock is still in his hand. His wrinkled brow shows how hard he is concentrating on what he's about to do.

When finished, the statue was the talk of Florence. What a wonder it was! Originally, it was meant to be placed on the front of the cathedral, forty feet off the ground. But at that height it would be difficult to see from the ground. It was agreed that the statue deserved a more important location. So David was moved to a central square of the city. For four hundred years he remained there, a proud symbol of Florence's independence. Today David is in a museum in Florence, protected from the weather.

What did Leonardo think of sculptors?

Not much. Leonardo didn't think of them as real artists. He said all they did was hammer away at rock, getting sweaty and completely covered in marble powder so that they looked like common bakers.

What did Michelangelo think of painters?

Not much. He thought painting was too easy. Nevertheless, in 1508, he began covering the ceiling of the pope's private chapel in Rome with more than eleven thousand square feet of frescoes. Did Michelangelo take the job because the pope practically ordered him to? Or did Michelangelo's deep faith make him want to celebrate Christianity on a spectacular scale? Maybe it was for both reasons.

Painting the ceiling of the Sistine Chapel was an enormous undertaking and a dangerous one, too. Michelangelo had to work seventy feet above the floor. For a long time it was believed that he did the frescoes lying on a scaffold, with paint dripping down all over him. But that's not true. He worked standing on a platform, constantly craning his neck to see what he was doing. Because of this, he suffered from terrible neck pain for the rest of his life.

At the end of four exhausting years, the ceiling was completed. There were nine scenes from the Bible, starting with the creation of the world and ending with the story of Noah and the flood. The most recognized moment, now seen on millions of posters and postcards, is when God extends his hand to Adam, bringing him to life.

The *Creation of Adam*

In all, Michelangelo painted more than three hundred figures on the ceiling of the Sistine Chapel, each one exhibiting massive strength and power.

(Just as Leonardo had, Michelangelo dissected bodies to better understand how to make the people in his paintings look real.)

Michelangelo was making drawings for future projects until eight days before he died in 1564. He was eighty-eight years old.

So who was the greater genius? Leonardo or Michelangelo?

Undoubtedly, each would have said "Me!"

CHAPTER 6
A New Way of Building

The paintings, frescoes, and statues of the Renaissance were most often commissioned for important churches or privately owned palaces. Like the artwork displayed inside them, buildings of the 1400s and 1500s were very different from those of the Middle Ages.

Renaissance architecture in many ways was an example of the old being new again. Columns with decorated capitals (tops), rows of arches, and domes all came back in style. These design elements hadn't appeared on buildings for a thousand years. But Renaissance architects wanted to achieve the same sense of order and balance found in the landmarks of the classical past.

Columns frame a Renaissance courtyard

This Medici palace was built in 1444. The design of its dark stone facade (front) is symmetrical. Symmetry was a common feature in Renaissance architecture. It means the left and right sides mirror each other. The palace was built around a square garden with statues. Although the Medici palace looks forbidding— it was originally built as a fortress—the rooms inside were the height of luxury.

Filippo Brunelleschi of Florence is considered the first architect of the Renaissance. For many years, he and his friend Donatello lived in Rome.

Filippo Brunelleschi

They visited ruins and studied ancient buildings and sculpture there. What most awed Brunelleschi was the Pantheon, an ancient Roman temple. It was in the shape of a square, topped with a circular dome.

The Pantheon

The great cathedral in Florence, which was begun in 1296, still needed a dome. Although he had no training in architecture, Brunelleschi won the commission to build the dome. He did it by using his wits.

Brunelleschi asked the committee in charge

a single question: If he could stand an egg on a table, would they give him the job?

Make an egg stand up? That was impossible.

So the committee told Brunelleschi to go ahead and try.

All it took was carefully and gently cracking the bottom of the egg before placing it upright. Brunelleschi got the job!

Now that he had the commission came the hard part—actually building the brick dome.

Small domes could be constructed using a wooden framework placed on the inside. However, the Florence cathedral's dome would be one hundred and thirty-six feet across. There wasn't enough timber in the area for a framework that big. But without this support, a heavy dome would collapse under its own weight.

From his knowledge of math and geometry, Brunelleschi came up with a brilliant idea. He decided to build two lightweight domes, one fitting inside the other, like two nesting eggs. Having two lighter domes meant there wasn't as much weight bearing down on the structure. This lessened the stress on the building.

Work started in 1420.

With the crew working from the outside, circular layers of bricks were laid to start the inner dome. Each layer rested on the one below and slanted a little more inward. As the work progressed, the circles of bricks got smaller and smaller until the dome was finished. Then the outer dome was built in the same way. For support, nine horizontal stone rings held each dome in place, like metal bands around a barrel. There were also vertical "ribs" for support that met at the top of the dome. Brunelleschi even invented special cranes for lifting supplies up to the crew working hundreds of feet off the ground.

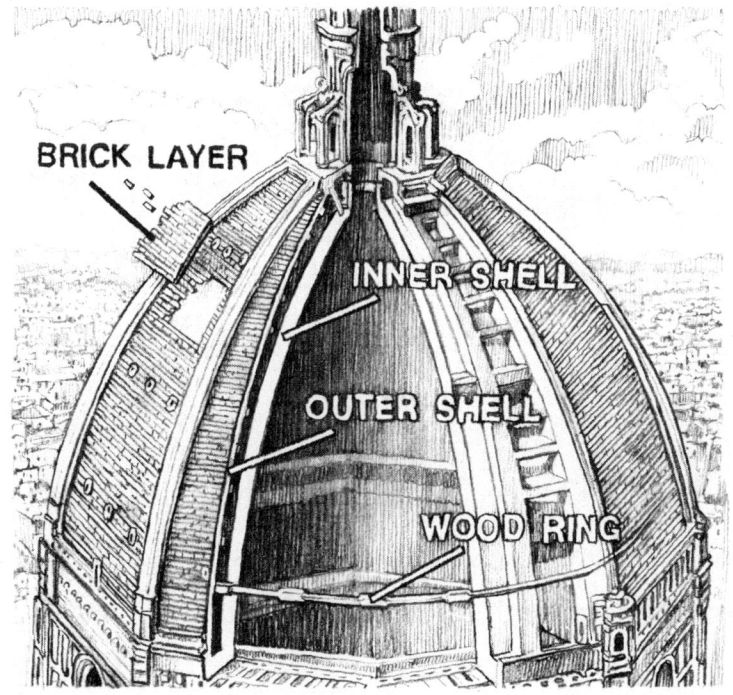

BRICK LAYER

INNER SHELL

OUTER SHELL

WOOD RING

Brunelleschi's majestic redbrick dome became the wonder of Florence. It still can be seen from all parts of the city. When he died in 1446, Brunelleschi was buried beneath it and rests there to this day.

Florence Cathedral

In 1547, seventy-one-year-old Michelangelo built an even bigger dome. (Yes, Michelangelo was an incredible architect, too.) It was for

St. Peter's Basilica, the largest church in the world. It was part of the Catholic Church's plan to return Rome to its glory days. The pope wanted the city to outshine Florence. Since he was the ruler of Rome as well as the head of the Church, he had the money to do it. This period, when Rome overtook Florence as the center for art and architecture, is known as the High Renaissance.

Saint Peter's Basilica, Rome

Building the dome was the last commission of Michelangelo's life. He worked on it for eighteen years. The height of the black letters in Latin that go around the inside of the base gives a sense of the dome's size. Each is six feet high. The Bible verse they spell out is: *You are Peter, and on this rock I will build my church and give you the keys to the kingdom of heaven.* This is a reference to Saint Peter, one of Jesus's followers. He is considered the first pope of the Catholic Church.

At its top point, the dome is three hundred and sixty feet off the floor. That's as high as a thirty-five-story skyscraper! Looking up at it is an almost overwhelming experience. Yet Michelangelo always said that Brunelleschi's dome was more beautiful.

CHAPTER 7
A Renaissance in the North

The countries of northern Europe (Belgium, Germany, the Netherlands) also contributed in major ways to the Renaissance. It was in

Germany, after all, that the printing press was developed.

Although there weren't great sculptors or architects on par with the ones in Italy, there were spectacular painters in northern Europe. Their work had a brand-new realism, but of a different kind.

Northern artists could render objects in such detail that their works looked like photographs. A painting called the *Annunciation Triptych* by the workshop of Robert Campin shows an angel telling Mary that she will become the mother of Jesus. It was painted between 1427 and 1432 in the Netherlands. The scene takes place in the sitting room of a middle-class home. The tabletop tilts at an odd angle. The bench by the fireplace isn't in correct proportion to the rest of the room. It's way too long. But the details in the picture are extraordinarily realistic. The painted vase holding flowers looks like genuine glazed pottery.

The bronze kettle gleams and reflects light the way real metal would. And the smoke curls from the candle exactly how it would after the flame's been snuffed out.

Middle panel of the *Annunciation Triptych*

How did artists like Campin achieve these miraculous special effects?

With oil paint.

Italian artists used paint that had an egg base. Called tempera, this type of paint dried quickly and created a flat, solid surface. Paint with an oil base (often made from linseed, also known as flax) could be made in a wide variety of colors. Using paintbrushes with no more than one or two bristles, artists worked slowly, dabbing on one tiny speck of paint over another to create extraordinarily realistic effects.

To show off the magical illusions they could create, northern European artists sometimes would include a mirror in a painting, reflecting a miniature scene inside it.

One such painting is the portrait of a newly married couple painted by Jan van Eyck in 1434. Born in Belgium, he was a master of Northern Renaissance art. The mirror takes up only a little bit of space in the painting. But a very close look at it reveals not only the back of the newlyweds but also the artist himself painting the picture!

The Arnolfini Portrait by Jan van Eyck

Van Eyck also signed his name in large letters across the top—Jan van Eyck was here—as if he'd been a witness at the wedding.

The German artist Hans Holbein the Younger spent many years working in England. He became known as the painter of royalty because he made so many portraits of the kings and queens of Europe.

Until the Renaissance, portraits—paintings of actual people—were uncommon. During the Middle Ages, sometimes a wealthy family would buy a painting of a religious event, such as the birth of Jesus, and ask the artist to add them into the scene. Having their likenesses

Hans Holbein

included was a way of showing they were people of strong religious faith. But the family would be painted off to the side and much smaller in size than the important holy figures in the scene.

Now, however, rich people felt that they were important enough to deserve full-size paintings of just themselves and their families.

Holbein painted a famous portrait of King Henry VIII. The way Henry stands with his legs apart and his hands on his hips in the painting makes it clear just how powerful he was. Nobody wanted to mess with him!

Soon after Henry's third wife died in 1537, he wanted to get married again. Princess Anne of Cleves, in Germany, seemed like a good choice. Henry sent Hans Holbein to paint her portrait so he could see what she looked like. (This was three hundred years before photography.)

Holbein returned to England with a full-length portrait of a beautiful princess. And Henry agreed to marry her. But when she arrived, he was very disappointed! To the king, Anne looked different from the princess in Holbein's painting.

Henry and Anne were married, and then quickly divorced. The king was not pleased with Hans Holbein. The painter was lucky to keep his head!

During the Northern Renaissance, everyday life also came to be seen as a worthy subject of oil painting. Ordinary people are shown baking bread, taking a nap, or sitting by a fire to stay warm. One painting by Pieter Brueghel, the Elder (c. 1525–1569) of the Netherlands shows many children playing all sorts of games.

They blow bubbles, turn somersaults, do handstands, ride hobby horses, walk on stilts, roll hoops. About eighty different games have been identified in the painting, many of them still played today. It was painted in 1560 and is called *Children's Games*.

Although finished more than four hundred years ago, the painting is a reminder that in some ways the world hasn't changed all that much since the Renaissance.

CHAPTER 8
The Heavens Above

During the Renaissance, there came to be a new and completely different understanding of Earth's place in the universe. It caused a lot of controversy.

Until the 1500s, Earth was believed to be the center of the universe, staying in one place

and never moving. People thought the six known planets circled it. This idea dated back to the time of Ptolemy (c. 100–170), a mathematician and astronomer of ancient Egypt.

Ptolemy

The Catholic Church approved of Ptolemy's geocentric (Earth-centered) system of the universe because it backed up the stories in the Bible. If God had created Earth, of course it would have a special importance in the universe.

Nicolaus Copernicus (1473–1543) was an astronomer from Poland, in northern Europe. He had read the works of Aristarchus, an ancient Greek astronomer who believed that Earth and the other planets revolved around the sun. Using

Nicolaus Copernicus

mathematical principles and observing how the planets moved in the sky, Copernicus believed Aristarchus was right. Earth did not appear to be the center of the universe after all. He also began to understand that Earth turned daily on its axis.

Copernicus was an official in the Catholic Church. He knew how opposed the Church would be to his ideas. He understood that he might even be put in prison for them. So the

A page from
On the Revolutions of the Heavenly Spheres

book he wrote about his findings, called *On the Revolutions of the Heavenly Spheres*, was kept secret for decades. Only a few other astronomers knew about it. (And most of them didn't agree with Copernicus.) It wasn't until after he died in 1543 that his book was finally published. It was too late by then for the Church to punish him.

More than sixty years later, another astronomer backed up what Copernicus had discovered. His name was Galileo Galilei (1564–1642), and he worked in Florence. He had learned about telescopes, which were invented by Dutch eyeglass makers.

Using a telescope of his own construction, Galileo was able to see much more than Copernicus had using only his eyes. Galileo observed that the moon was not flat or smooth.

The First Telescope

In 1608, Hans Lippershey, a German man who made glass lenses in Holland, was watching two children play in his shop. By placing two different-shaped glass lenses together, they were able to clearly see a weathervane on top of a building far away. The children were only having fun, but they gave Lippershey a great idea for an invention that could magnify objects at three times their normal size.

It is believed that Lippershey invented one of the first telescopes.

It was a sphere with mountains and bowl-shaped depressions called craters.

In 1610, he wrote *Starry Messenger* about his new observations. The book became quite popular. Now the notion of a heliocentric (sun-centered) universe became widely known.

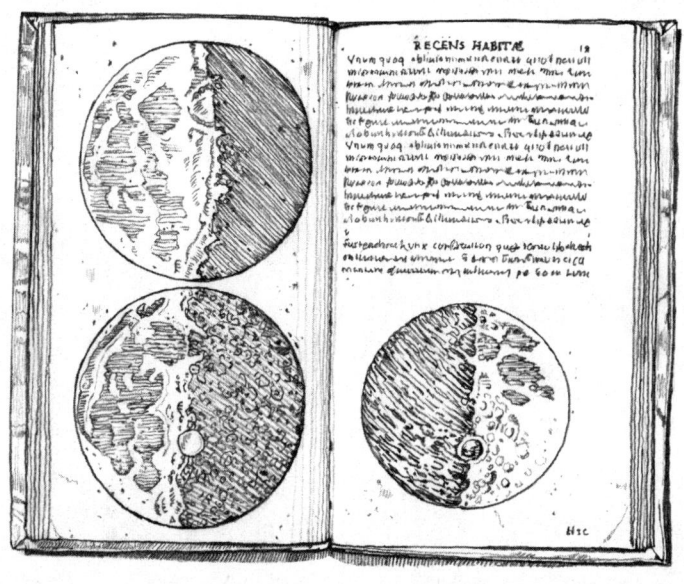

A page from *Starry Messenger*

Galileo was braver than Copernicus. But Copernicus had been right to worry about the

Church's reaction. Galileo was put on trial in 1633 in Rome and sentenced to house arrest for the rest of his life.

As for Copernicus, for centuries his body lay buried in an unmarked grave in Frombork Cathedral, in Poland. It was not until 2005, through DNA comparisons, that his remains were identified and later reburied in the cathedral with a proper tombstone that shows a golden sun surrounded by planets.

CHAPTER 9
The World Grows Larger

Ideas about what the Earth itself looked like were changing rapidly. This was because the Renaissance was an age of tremendous exploration.

Were explorers of the 1400s and 1500s searching for unknown lands solely for the thrill of adventure? Or because of their interest in geography?

Neither. They were looking to make money. Lots of it.

Living in palaces with spectacular artwork was only part of the good life for the rich during the Renaissance. They dressed in beautiful clothes, wore fabulous jewelry, and feasted on delicious food. However, many luxury items couldn't be found in Western Europe. Silks, precious gems, and spices had to be brought all the way from lands known as the Far East. That made them very expensive. At one point an ounce of pepper cost as much as an ounce of gold.

Why were spices so desirable and so expensive?

For one thing, spices—salt, pepper, cinnamon, nutmeg—made food tastier. Also, coating meat and fish in salt kept them from spoiling quickly. That was important in a time without refrigeration. Unfortunately, Western Europe didn't have the right climate for growing spices. They had to be imported (brought in) from the Far East.

Getting from Western Europe to the Far East by land was no easy trip. It took many months and was dangerous. Travelers had to cross mountains, endure extreme weather, and avoid murderous bands of robbers.

Like Florence and Milan, Venice was another important city-state in Italy. Its location in a lagoon on the Northern Adriatic Sea made it the best starting point from which to set out for the Far East.

The long journey was first made in 1271. A seventeen-year-old Venetian named Marco Polo traveled to China with his father and uncle, who were merchants. Marco Polo spent twenty years in China (then called Cathay). He wrote a book that told of the wonders he saw there.

The Travels of Marco Polo became a medieval best seller. It spurred other Italian merchants to travel to the Far East and bring back luxury goods to sell and profit from.

Then, in 1453, the Turkish Empire, which surrounded Constantinople on both sides, captured the city.

The fall of Constantinople was terrible news for Italian merchants. The city was the first stop on the long trip to the Far East. Now foreigners entering Constantinople had to pay taxes. The extra cost meant there'd be less profit made on goods brought back to sell in Europe.

Another route to the Far East needed to be found.

Prince Henry of Portugal (1394–1460) thought an ocean-going route might be the answer. Portugal, unlike Italy, was on the coast of the Atlantic Ocean. The Portuguese were known for being

Prince Henry of Portugal

expert sailors. Still, voyages by sea to the Far East would require sailing all the way around the continent of Africa and then farther on to the Indies. (The Indies was the name for China and Japan as well as India.) This had never been done. So far, Italy had controlled foreign trading. Prince Henry wanted Portugal to become a key player in Far Eastern trade, too. Maybe now was the time to try.

During the Renaissance period, ships became lighter and maps became more accurate. There were also improved instruments such as the magnetic compass and the quadrant. They helped sailors figure out their location on the open seas where all they could see was water, water, and more water.

The Portuguese prince never went to sea himself. Still, he became known as Henry the Navigator because he paid for so many voyages along the coast of Africa.

Caravels

In Portugal by the mid-1400s, shipbuilders were making a new vessel that was better equipped for long voyages: the caravel. With a new system of multiple sails and masts, these boats could deal with all kinds of winds. And because caravels weighed less than older ships, they also moved through the water faster. They could make long trips in less time.

Caravels were used by both Spanish and Portuguese sailors and explorers.

By 1460, after Prince Henry had died, ships reached Sierra Leone. A trading center was established there. Still more voyages continued, making their way farther and farther down the African coast. In 1488, Bartolomeu Dias sailed around the southern tip of Africa and out into the Indian Ocean. At last, ten years later, Vasco da Gama reached the west coast of India!

King Ferdinand and Queen Isabella of Spain

Christopher Columbus

had been watching the success of Portugal with envy. They hired an Italian sailor who had a new plan for reaching the Indies. His name was Christopher Columbus.

Instead of sailing all the way around Africa, Columbus wanted to sail directly west across the Atlantic. He believed this way of reaching the Indies would take much less time. That was because he thought Spain and China were only about 2,300 miles apart. But he was wrong. No map of the time showed that two continents—North and South America—lay in between Europe and the Far East. The real distance was 12,000 miles.

In early August 1492, three ships under his command set out from Spain. Two months later, land was spotted. The Indies! Columbus was sure of that. But in reality, he had reached the Bahamas! Later on, he made three more voyages across the Atlantic Ocean. He died still certain that he had reached the Far East.

Later voyages by explorers to what was incorrectly called "the New World" brought untold riches to certain countries in Europe. But it was a disaster for the people who had been living in these lands for centuries. Entire civilizations—the Inca, the Aztec, and many others—were wiped out. They were murdered by the European explorers or died from diseases carried and spread by them. The crime of trafficking in human lives also began. Slavery in the New World lasted until the end of the American Civil War in 1865.

By the early 1500s, the size of the known world had tripled! That's why the Renaissance is also rightfully called the Age of Exploration.

Map of the Americas, 1500s

CHAPTER 10
A Giant Leap Forward

The Renaissance was without question a remarkable era. But was life better for everyone?

No. Mostly just for the rich and the powerful.

Cities were growing. In the fifteenth century, Florence was home to sixty thousand people. Venice's population was double that size. There was a growing middle class of well-off craftsmen and merchants and shopkeepers. But cities were filthy and overcrowded. There were few sources of fresh water and no sewer systems. Garbage collected in ditches in the streets. Diseases spread quickly.

But 90 percent of Europe's population still lived in the countryside. Peasants (poor farmers) scraped by, farming plots of land that belonged to the local lord. Their homes were simple huts.

No one ever traveled more than a few miles away to the nearest village on market days. When crops failed, peasants struggled just to stay alive.

By 1600, printing presses had been turning out books for more than one hundred and fifty years. Yet only about 20 percent of the people in Europe could read.

Nevertheless, during the Renaissance there was a great leap forward in so many areas, including

in art, architecture, and astronomy. Humanism had brought about a whole new way of thinking about life. People came to realize that they could do great things—create new inventions, explore new continents—and began to understand Earth's place in the universe. All this happened during the Renaissance, which led to the modern world we know today.

Timeline of the Renaissance

1271	Marco Polo, along with his father and uncle, leaves Venice for the Far East
1304	Petrarch, one of the early humanists, is born
1420	Brunelleschi begins building the dome of Florence Cathedral
c. 1435	Donatello sculpts a free-standing statue of David
1440	Johannes Gutenberg invents a printing press with movable type
1453	The city of Constantinople is conquered by the Turks
1503	Leonardo da Vinci begins painting the *Mona Lisa*
1504	Michelangelo finishes his seventeen-foot-tall statue of David
1512	Michelangelo completes the frescoes on the ceiling of the Sistine Chapel in Rome
1519	Leonardo dies in France
1535	Humanist Thomas More of England is beheaded on orders of King Henry VIII
1543	Nicolaus Copernicus dies
1564	Michelangelo dies at age eighty-eight
1608	Hans Lippershey invents a telescope
1610	Astronomer Galileo Galilei publishes *Starry Messenger*
2005	Copernicus's remains are identified using DNA

Timeline of the World

1313 — New printing techniques using characters carved from wood are developed in China

1320 — The Aztecs begin building their capital city, Tenochtitlan, in what is now Mexico

1347 — The bubonic plague reaches Europe, killing millions

1387– 1400 — Geoffrey Chaucer writes the collection of stories known as *The Canterbury Tales*

1407 — A public bank is founded in Genoa, Italy

1429 — Joan of Arc leads French troops against the English

1472 — The city of Amsterdam bans snowball fights

1488 — The Great Wall of China is extended

1501 — Amerigo Vespucci determines that Columbus had actually reached a new continent, later named North America

1509 — Henry VIII is crowned king of England

1522 — Explorer Ferdinand Magellan's ship is first to sail around the world

1550 — Chocolate is introduced in Europe

1564 — William Shakespeare is born in Stratford-upon-Avon, England

2008 — Barack Obama becomes the first African American to be elected president of the United States

Bibliography

*Books for young readers

*Anderson, Kristen. *Who Was Michelangelo?* New York: Penguin Random House, 2022.

*Daly, Catherine. *What Was the Age of Exploration?* New York: Penguin Random House, 2021.

*Holub, Joan. *Who Was Marco Polo?* New York: Penguin Random House, 2007.

Isaacson, Walter. *Leonardo da Vinci*. New York: Simon & Schuster, 2017.

King, Ross. *Brunelleschi's Dome: How a Renaissance Genius Reinvented Architecture*. New York: Bloomsbury USA, 2013.

*McLanathan, Richard. *Leonardo da Vinci*. New York: Harry N. Abrams, 1990.

Snyder, James. *Northern Renaissance Art: Painting, Sculpture, the Graphic Arts from 1350 to 1575*. New York: Harry N. Abrams, 1985.

Suh, H. Anna, ed. *Leonardo's Notebooks: Writing and Art of the Great Master*. New York: Black Dog & Leventhal, Publishers, 2005.

*Wood, Tim. *The Renaissance*. New York: Viking Books, 1992.